Brian Webb & Peyton Skipwith

# David Gentleman
# **DESIGN**

Antique Collectors' Club

Design Series format by Brian Webb
Design: David Gentleman © 2009 Brian Webb and Peyton Skipwith
Foreword © 2009 Alan Bennett

ISBN 978-1-85149-595-5

British Library cataloguing-in-Publication Data
A catalogue record for this book is available from the British Library.

Antique Collectors' Club
www.antiquecollectorsclub.com

Sandy Lane, Old Martlesham,
Woodbridge, Suffolk IP12 4SD, UK
Tel: 01394 389950 Fax: 01394 389999
Email: info@antique-acc.com
or
116 Pleasant Street - Suite 18
Easthampton, MA 01027, USA
Tel: (413) 529 0861 Fax: (413) 529 0862
Email: sales@antiquecc.com

Picture credits
p.8 (below) Photograph: Hugh Gentleman, acknowledgements to
Hugh and Rosemary Gentleman
p.27 The Towner Museum and Gallery, Eastbourne
p.88 Photograph: Jess Hurd

The cover and endpapers are reproduced from
Saint George & the Dragon, 1973

Published by Antique Collectors' Club, Woodbridge, England
Design by Webb & Webb Design Limited, London
Printed and bound in China

# Foreword

When I was a child I thought there was something magical about people who could draw. A boy in my class could do horses and this seemed to me at eight or nine a gift that was almost celestial.

I was reminded of this recently seeing David Gentleman drawing in Inverness Street market: not an uncommon occurrence as David is as much a component of the Camden Town scene as the market itself. On this occasion though a little Asian boy was stationed right at his elbow rapt in what David was drawing while standing so close to him that he was almost impeding the process. I can imagine artists who would find this intolerable but that David didn't is evidence both of how gentle and good-natured he is but also of his belief in the learning process and how interest and even skill is acquired and passed on.

Though he has ranged the world in his subject matter David Gentleman seems to me despite his parents' Scottish origins to be a very English artist. I first became aware of modern British pictures and painting when as a boy in 1951 I was taken to the Festival of Britain. David was just too young to be one of the artists featured and employed there but his vision seems to me to be linked to and grow out of that magical time. To read the list of artists and craftsmen by whom he was taught or with whom he associated at the Royal College is mouth-watering. Peyton Skipwith calls it a veritable roll-call of the great and the good of the mid 20c British art world; in David Gentleman lives on the spirit of Bawden and John Nash.

And that's not all. The account of David's career reminds us of his extraordinary range. My own experience teaches me that the British don't really care for range; they think of it as inconsistency or want of application. A single furrow is better. Happily that's never been

David Gentleman's philosophy: postage stamps one assignment, a major Underground platform the next.

He has lived in the same street in Camden Town for the last fifty-odd years during which time, in the intervals of depicting France, Italy or India, he has recorded his immediate surroundings much as that other Camden Town painter William Roberts did but from a different perspectives (and without William Roberts' volleys of abuse!) And that's relevant. Art is never an excuse for bad behaviour. Talent isn't measurable by tantrums and I think again of his patience with that impromptu pupil in the market. I suppose what I'm saying is that David is a gentleman... or a gentleman twice over.

For myself I will always cherish the two sketches he did of Miss Shepherd, the Lady in the Van, a personage with whom he must have been almost as familiar as I was: we were all long term residents of our Camden Town street. In her time Miss Shepherd went through several vehicles and on one occasion David did a quick thumbnail sketch of Miss Shepherd watching as the tow truck prepared to take away her derelict van. He caught her in a familiar pose, feet splayed out in her version of ballet's No.1 position and so exactly that when Maggie Smith played Miss Shepherd on the stage I was able to show her the sketch so that she knew how to stand.

The other drawing is posthumous, done just a few days after Miss Shepherd died. I was working at my table in the window when I became aware of David casually leaning against the wall recording the van, now bowered in trees, which had been both Miss Shepherd's home and her catafalque. When he'd done he came in and gave me it.

Alan Bennett

Three Tuscan Towers from David Gentleman's Italy, 1997.

# Design
# David Gentleman

*In his inaugural address as Master of the Faculty of Royal Designers for Industry in November 1989, David Gentleman said 'the idea of drawing and designing represents and puts in a nutshell, as it were, those two opposites, Art and Industry'.*

None of the previous artists whose work Brian Webb and I have looked at in this *Design* series – Edward Bawden, Eric Ravilious, the Nash brothers and McKnight Kauffer – or the many who worked with the Curwen Press, including David's father, Tom Gentleman, seem to have felt the need to analyse and rationalise the differences, however minute, that separated their design work from their activities as painters and draughtsmen. That Gentleman felt this need in 1989 was, in part, a response to his audience, but also owed something to the fact that he grew up in a home in which art and design were regular topics of conversation. His father, Tom (1892-1966), was a painter who, due to the necessity of earning a living, became a graphic designer, while his mother, Winifred (1899-1966), put aside her own career to look after the family and augmented her creative urge through hand-loom weaving.

David, who was born in 1930, and his brother, Hugh, were brought up in Hertford, but David's parents met as fellow students at Glasgow School of Art immediately after the First World War. Their own family backgrounds had been very different from the aesthetically aware home life in rural England that they were able to give their two sons. Tom's father, William, owned a draper's shop in Coatbridge, Lanarkshire – then a depressed, and depressing, coal and steel town, where art was virtually an unknown world; Winfred's father, William Murgatroyd, was an accountant. Despite the fact that Tom had some modest success as a painter, he was unable to earn a living by it, so he and Winifred moved south to

Poster by Tom Gentleman, c1938.

Table Napkin for *Ashley
and Margaret Havinden*
by Winifred Gentleman,
1965.

Hertford, within easy commuting distance of London, where he was able to get design work at the various advertising agencies. The first of these was Benson's, where Dorothy L Sayers was employed as a copywriter, and Bobby Bevan (son of the painter Robert Bevan) dreamt up the famous slogan 'Guinness is Good for You'. Tom Gentleman later worked at Crawford's and at Stuart's before finding a permanent billet as chief artist in the design studio at Shell, where he was in regular contact with some of the finest designers of the day, including McKnight Kauffer and Barnett Freedman. This was the heyday of the poster and Tom Gentleman, a committed Modernist, was at the top of the profession and able to make a valuable contribution to this popular art form. Shell-Mex & BP Ltd, under the enlightened guidance of Jack Beddington, and the London Passenger Transport Board, under Frank Pick, were at the time the two largest and most adventurous commissioners of posters and other illustrated promotional material in Britain.

Although working as a designer, Tom Gentleman continued throughout his life to regard himself primarily as a painter. David recalls his father commuting to London four days a week and devoting the other three to painting and gardening; his studio being the greenhouse at their home – which, with nostalgia for his parents' native Scotland, and given its island site, was named 'Fair Isle'. Fair Isle had an orchard and large garden surrounded by the River Beane, which was a natural haven for swans and their cygnets. For David, who was visually aware and had a retentive memory, the impression of these bucolic surroundings was greatly enhanced when his father returned one day bearing the five volume set of Thomas Bewick's engravings. To this day Bewick remains one of his heroes, and these volumes sit on his shelves alongside the many books he himself has written or illustrated. In fact Bewick's example was in many ways the springboard for David's own career, inspiring him at the age of seventeen to go to St Albans Art School where, among other disciplines, he studied wood engraving. In common with other teenagers in those immediate postwar years, his studies were interrupted by two

years' national service, during which time he became a sergeant
in the Education Corps and was lucky enough to find himself in
charge of an art room in a camp on the edge of Bodmin Moor.
The sergeants' mess was soon enlivened by the first of David
Gentleman's murals, to be followed, after he was demobbed,
by another in a local Hertfordshire school.

A vital part of the postwar reconstruction of Britain was the
building of new schools and hospitals, and the Labour Government,
under Clement Atlee, channelled much of the country's scarce
financial resources into this work. Educationally, Hertfordshire
was one of the most enlightened English counties, and its education
officer, John Newsom, in conjunction with the Architectural
Department of the County Council commissioned a number of
architect-designed, system-built schools. In contrast to the surviving
grim, red brick, Victorian Board Schools, these new buildings were
intended to be full of light and optimism, and murals were an
integral part of the plan. Apart from David – who took a local theme,
Barnet Fair, for his mural – other artists who benefited from this
enlightened scheme included Julian Trevelyan and Prunella Clough.

In the autumn of 1950 he went to the Royal College of Art
in Kensington, at that time enjoying a renaissance under its
ambitious young rector, Robin Darwin. Unusually for the time,
as far as the College was concerned, money was not a constraint,
and the various tutors and departmental heads were encouraged
by Darwin to apply for any equipment they required. Whilst
Professor Guyatt was acquiring new printing presses for the
School of Graphic Design, a newly established department, to
which Gentleman was assigned, the austere and perverse Edward
Bawden merely indented for 'an adequate supply of candles', on
the basis that candlelight was very good for drawing by. The
following year he switched courses from graphic design to
illustration; resuming the study of wood engraving, this time
under that minor master of the medium, John Nash. Between
these two disciplines he came in contact with some of Britain's

finest artists and designers, many of whom were then teaching at the College.

Although Darwin may have had funds to spend on equipment, rationing was still in place and austerity remained the general rule, with the result that most artists relied on full- or part-time teaching to supplement their otherwise meagre incomes. The School of Graphic Design had as tutors, in addition to John Nash, the two Edwards – Bawden and Ardizzone – Reynolds Stone, Barnett Freedman, John Lewis, Abram Games and Henri Henrion, while the Painting School, (to which the illustrators had ready access), was taught by Colin Hayes, Ruskin Spear, Rodrigo Moynihan, Carel Weight, Robert Buhler, Kenneth Rowntree, John Minton and, occasionally, Henry Lamb. A veritable roll-call of the great and the good of the mid-twentieth century British art world. Gentleman and his fellow graphic students also had access to the letterpress printing department and Edwin La Dell's lithographic studio, facilities that few other colleges could emulate at that time. However, as he later recorded, 'the best thing about the College was the mixture of disciplines: in the students' common room at lunchtime one would meet people from the other schools: Pottery and Glass, Wood, Metals and Plastics, Furniture, Stained Glass, Textiles and Fashion.'[1] A very stimulating environment for a twenty year-old recently released from the Army.

Those first few years after the war were an extraordinary time to be a student. Despite the rationing, a range of new materials and fabrics, many of which had been developed for aeroplane manufacture, were gradually becoming available, and there were plenty of budding young designers clamouring to exploit them. The first big postwar exhibition of British manufactures, *Britain Can Make It* – or as Enid Marx called it, *Britain Can Make It, But Can't Have It* – was staged at the V&A in 1946, with queues of culture-starved visitors stretching the length of the Brompton Road as far as Harrods. The exhibits, however, were all for export, in order to bring in much-needed foreign currency. Five years later, by which

*Wood engravings from A Tale of Two Swannes
by W Vallans, Lion and Unicorn Press, 1953.*

time David was already at the College, the country, and London in particular, joined in celebration with the Festival of Britain. Many of the tutors, as well as some of the third-year students, were caught up in the creative ferment of the Festival.

Partly in response to the Festival, with its Lion and Unicorn Pavilion, Richard Guyatt set up the College's own printing house, The Lion and the Unicorn Press, which, in 1953, published the first of Gentleman's illustrated books, *A Tale of Two Swannes*, an Elizabethan poem about the rivers of Hertfordshire, including the Beane, which flowed through the garden at Fair Isle. The following year Guyatt masterminded its most ambitious production, *Births, Marriages and Deaths*, which, as he explained in the introduction, consisted of a 'number of extracts from novels and biographies chosen to illustrate the themes of Birth, Marriage and Death.' David Gentleman chose as his contribution a chapter from Flaubert's *Madame Bovary*. As Guyatt went on to explain, the literary content of the book was not of prime importance, its main purpose being the actual production, carried through by second- and third-year students in the School of Graphic Design. The task had been set, he said, as a 'technical exercise to enable those students taking part – the illustrators, typographers, the designers and the bookbinders – to face the problems, both aesthetic and technical, which only arise in acute and realistic form with an actual production job. [...] It contains as many different methods of reproduction as the present printing facilities at the College allow.'[2]

David Gentleman, who by the time the book appeared had become a junior tutor at the College, decorated the title page of his section with a small vignette head of Madame Bovary and illustrated the text with six further wood engravings; other students opted for a variety of printing techniques including two-, three- and five-colour lithography, etching, line block, pochoir, sugar aquatint, linocut, half-tone block and three-colour Plastocowell – a process akin to lithography, developed by one of his tutors, John Lewis, at W.S. Cowell of Ipswich. In addition to the different techniques of reproduction, a similarly wide variety of type-faces and papers were employed. Gentleman's contribution was set in fourteen point Garamond and printed on suede Basingwerk. Only a hundred copies of the book were printed, and it remains today a fitting monument to Guyatt and his staff and the facilities they had built up at the College in those difficult years. At this time Gentleman further extended his experience by designing ceramics and posters, including that for the students' Coronation Year Exhibition at the V&A.

The first illustrated work for which he was paid was André Simon's *What about Wine?* Although, whilst still a schoolboy, he had earned five pounds making a meticulous drawing of a company logo to embellish a poster his father was working on for Pan Yan Pickle: a rushed freelance job from Ashley Havinden at Crawford's. David illustrated *What about Wine?* with engravings based on drawings made in France during College summer vacations. In his final year – by which time he had married fellow-student Rosalind Dease – David won a travelling scholarship enabling the couple to spend the summer in Italy. The sketchbooks he filled during these continental sojourns provided much of the source material for the drawings of peasant life with which he decorated a textile design for Edinburgh Weavers, as well as supplying much needed documentary information for the shopfronts, and estaminet interiors which, along with detailed studies of cuts of meat and varieties of fish and fungi, enliven the pages of Patience Gray's *Plats du Jour, or Foreign Food*, published in 1957. Since then food and wine have remained an agreeable source of subject matter with illustrations for Harvey's 1961 *Wine List*, and Brown and Pank's *Off the Shelf*, which, like *What about Wine?* had an introduction by André Simon. More recently he has added olive oil and wine labels to his gastronomic repertoire.

At this time he made his first venture into the theatre with a design for a mosaic, *Pallas Athene*, commissioned by Hugh Casson as an embellishment to one of his stage sets for George Devine's

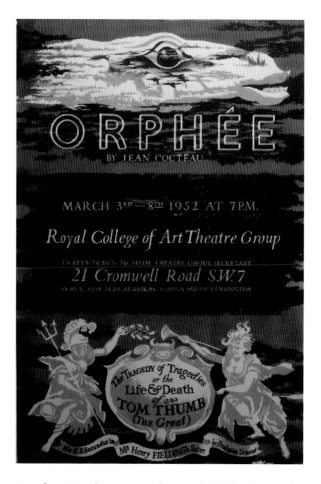

Poster for an RCA Theatre Group production, a double bill with Cocteau's play Orphée and Fielding's The Life and Death of Tom Thumb, 1952. This was the first of David Gentleman's many lithographs.

production of *Troilus and Cressida* at Covent Garden: with music
by William Walton, a cast that included Peter Pears and Geraint
Evans, and Malcolm Sargent conducting, its success was assured.
However, a couple of years later, in 1956, when he made a further
theatrical foray, he was not so lucky: *Roseland*, a musical play at
St Martin's Theatre for which he had designed the set, closed at
the end of its first week. Despite the fact this failure had nothing
to do with his set design, it is interesting to note that since then
Gentleman's work has been almost entirely two-dimensional
– chiefly book illustration, poster and stamp design, in addition to
his parallel career as draughtsman, watercolourist and printmaker.
It is perhaps because his work is so firmly drawing-based that,
given the rich and varied expertise amongst the Faculty of Royal
Designers for Industry (ranging from aerodynamics to the fashion
trade), he felt compelled in 1989 to attempt to identify the
difference between drawing and design. In his address he noted
that one of the dictionary definitions of design was 'purpose', and
in designing, he maintained, there was always a purpose – an
'intention'. What purpose, and whose, was another matter.

This question of whose purpose had been brought home to him
rather starkly some years previously when multinational chemicals
firm DuPont was sued following claims that its insecticide, Benlate,
caused blindness. David's beautiful engravings of fruit, flowers
and vegetables had adorned advertisements for Benlate in a variety
of farming and agricultural magazines. These engravings have an
affinity with some of the best of those of his erstwhile tutor, John
Nash, particularly, and ironically, his illustrations to *Poisonous Plants:
Deadly, Dangerous and Suspect*.

Until the mid-1960s most of the books that Gentleman illustrated,
including *The Swiss Family Robinson* for The Limited Editions Club
of New York, and John Clare's *The Shepherd's Calendar* , as well as the
thirty-two covers Hans Schmoller commissioned for the New
Penguin Shakespeare, were illustrated with wood engravings.
However, in *The Swiss Family Robinson*, he pushed beyond the usual

boundaries of the medium in order to achieve the effect he desired. He printed the engravings over brush-drawn backgrounds, giving them colour, variety and a sense of richness; a technique he had successfully exploited a few years previously in the Monotype Corporation's calendar 'The London Scene'. One outstanding exception to the use of wood engravings at this time is *Bridges on the Backs*, commissioned in 1961 by Brooke Crutchley as the Cambridge University Press's Christmas offering to its friends. This delightful conceit was designed to show the skills of the Press, and while some illustrations, such as those of the bridges at Clare and Queens' Colleges, are single sheets, others have one, two or even three overlays. The most elaborate of these is of the Garret Hostel Bridge, in which the illustration of the 1960 span bridge folds back to reveal its immediate predecessor, an 1830s cast-iron bridge, which, in turn reveals an even earlier wooden bridge. He had to draw each of these overlays as two- or four-colour separations.

Lithography was to become Gentleman's preferred method of illustration, with the result that three further books published by the Limited Editions Club – *Poems of John Keats* (1966), Kipling's *The Jungle Book* (1968) and *The Ballads of Robin Hood* (1977) – were illustrated in lush colour. Unlike engraving, drawing on a lithographic stone or zinc plate is akin to drawing on paper, the only major difference being the care needed to ensure that the different plates register one with another. Preparatory to illustrating *The Jungle Book*, and with the purpose of getting identifiable settings and local colour, Gentleman made the first of many trips to India. Whilst there he wrote several letters to his editor in New York, extracts from which were published in the Club's Monthly Newsletter. 'I am deep in Kipling's jungle,' he wrote, 'about fifteen miles from the road on a jungle forest track. I am writing by an oil lamp in the still very hot evening soon after sunset.' He went on to comment on the stillness of the birds, the sound of the crickets, the river where tigers, panther and deer drank, and the bleating of a distant goat, continuing, 'There is a woodland path where a dozen monkeys were leaping about this

The Grasshopper and Cricket, from The Poems of John Keats, *Limited Editions Club*, 1966.

morning, apparently waiting to be noticed, but slightly more appealing perhaps than the scoundrelly creatures of *The Jungle Book*.'[3] Although printed at the Stinehour Press in Vermont, *The Jungle Book* was designed by John Dreyfus of the Cambridge University Press, while the plates – ten colours plus black – were printed at Cowell's. Trade editions of these works, using a restricted number of colours, were produced by the Heritage Press, and comparison between them is instructive. Gentleman's puritanical spirit abhors excess and consequently a number of the plates in both these books are far more effective in four rather than ten colours. This is particularly true of the Kipling for which he had drawn the preliminary sketches in inks, giving an aniline harshness to the illustrations; the suppression, especially of the acid green, in the cheaper edition is definitely an improvement. The artwork for *Poems of John Keats* was softer, being done in watercolour, but here too the limitation of plates is often to advantage visually.

The four children's books he produced in 1967, variously depicting his eldest daughter's holiday activities in Greece, Spain, Ireland and the South of France, presage his own eponymous illustrated travelogues of the 1980s and '90s in Britain, France, Italy and India. These latter gave him the opportunity not only to travel and record places and scenes that he loves, but also to be seriously involved, as author, artist and designer, in every process of bookmaking. The elephant endpapers for *David Gentleman's India* have the joyous deligh of Jean de Brunhoff's Babar, without the anthropomorphic overtones.

Whatever the job in hand, Gentleman eschews self-indulgence, seeming to enjoy the act of paring away surplus detail in order to get at the essence of his subject; he adheres instinctively to McKnight Kauffer's dictum 'if in doubt leave it out.' Tautness and absence of clutter are the principal hallmarks of his work. In 1972 he wrote a book, *Design in Miniature*, in which he said that to design in miniature involves considerably more than just a simple matter of size or skill: 'An Elizabethan miniature by Hilliard is very different from a life-size portrait reduced to the same scale, for the size forces the artist to be extremely selective and to be quite ruthless in cutting out the inessentials. This makes for the characteristic intensity and clarity of design in miniature; compression in space giving the same unity as compression of time does in the classical theatre.'[4]

In his own work, Gentleman retains the characteristic intensity of the miniaturist even when it is enlarged. The discipline instilled by his early training engraving designs on small boxwood blocks ensures that whatever the task, the resulting design is always tight. Although much of his work, particularly the postage stamps and wine labels, is small in scale, he can, when required, turn his mind and hand to the monumental, as witness the hundred metre-long mural panels for Charing Cross Underground Station.

These panels, which were commissioned by London Transport in 1979 to decorate the north- and southbound platforms of the newly-rebuilt Northern Line at Charing Cross Underground Station, are the most dramatic example, in terms of Gentleman's work, of how a dauntingly large scheme can successfully be conceived in miniature. His brief was simply to create a tableau conveying some sense of the original Charing Cross – the last in a series series of crosses which King Edward I caused to be erected in memory of his wife, Eleanor of Castile. Queen Eleanor had died at Harby in Nottinghamshire and each cross marked one of the twelve places where her coffin rested during its progress to London. Gentleman decided to adopt a frieze format and to create a mural depicting the mediaeval workmen who built Eleanor's Cross. For those travellers today who have time to linger and study the mural, it illustrates the thirteenth-century building sequence from quarrymen to master mason, and the many skills involved.

Combining historical research with observation of present-day stonemasons and other craftsmen, Gentleman first developed his ideas as pencil sketches that he then refined and engraved on woodblocks, which, in turn, were printed on fibrous Japanese paper, specially chosen to give added texture. The printed images were then enlarged twenty-fold onto clear film and printed by silk screen onto metre-wide sections of melanine laminate.

Complex as this may sound, it only reflects the creative process and the mechanics of bringing the mural to fruition. In reality, of course, it was considerably more complicated, because long walls beside the platforms are not just flat surfaces, they are intersected by entrances and exits, as well as being interrupted by benches, notice-boards, the ubiquitous Underground logo, and, in the more peaceable days of the 1970s when the Charing Cross mural was executed, litter bins and staff letterboxes. As the position of each these was predetermined, Gentleman worked directly from the architect's blueprints, which enabled him to take into account these various impediments and make a virtue of them. Sadly, some of his inventiveness is now lost as the bins and boxes have, of necessity, been boarded over, whilst the thoughtless replacement of the wooden benches with articulated metal seats was an act of aesthetic vandalism. Gentleman had wittily incorporated the form of these benches into his artistic scheme, exploiting their simple shape in such a way that the mediaeval masons appeared to make use of them, sitting on them, resting their tools on them, and even wheeling their barrows along them, thus adding an extra dimension to this animated frieze of figures.

In preparing his original drawings, and the subsequent engravings, a further critical restriction arose when Gentleman realised that it was necessary to avoid sensitive parts of the design, especially faces, from overlapping from one panel onto another. However, it is overcoming such challenges that constitute the core of his philosophical belief that design equates with purpose.

Designing stamps or coins is at the opposite end of the scale in terms of size, but poses just as many problems. Gentleman has carried out numerous jobs for the Royal Mail and a few for the Royal Mint. The first set of stamps he was commissioned to design was in 1962 to celebrate the rather unpropitious theme of National Productivity Year. The powers-that-be who dreamt up this worthy initiative had devised a logo incorporating an upward-pointing arrow; the challenge for Gentleman was to include this logo, along with the Queen's head, the monetary denomination of each stamp, and the words 'National Productivity Year', plus the requirement to create some striking pictorial or graphic motif of his own. No easy task. The measure of how successfully he overcame the problem is that still, nearly half a century later, the designs remain attractive, fresh and fit for purpose. This success led to many further commissions celebrating themes as diverse as the ninth centenary of the Battle of Hastings, the life of Winston Churchill, the investiture of the Prince of Wales, Shakespeare's quatercentenary and Concorde. Individual designs have ranged from ones of considerable complexity, such as those for the Shakespeare and Battle of Hastings sets, to the pared-down simplicity of the Concorde images. He has said that designing stamps taught him a lot, 'not just about squeezing pictures and ideas into a small space, but about design and determination, and how improbable things could be made to happen.'[5] One such improbable thing was the commission from Anthony Wedgwood Benn, the Postmaster General, to produce an album of one hundred designs demonstrating how stamps could be used not just to mark specific events and anniversaries, but to reflect all things British – history, architecture, the arts, natural history, engineering and so on.

The necessity for the ruthless suppression of detail inherent in stamp design brought home to him in a practical way the difference between emblems, symbols and pictures – a lesson he has since exploited to good effect for both coinage and posters. Only two of his coin designs have been struck, a £5 piece in 2004 marking the centenary of the Entente Cordiale, and a £2 coin celebrating the bicentenary in 2007 of the abolition of slavery. The former incorporates, in a most ingenious manner, the twin images of Oscar Roty's *La Semeuse*, which adorned French stamps and coinage for some twenty years during the early part of the last

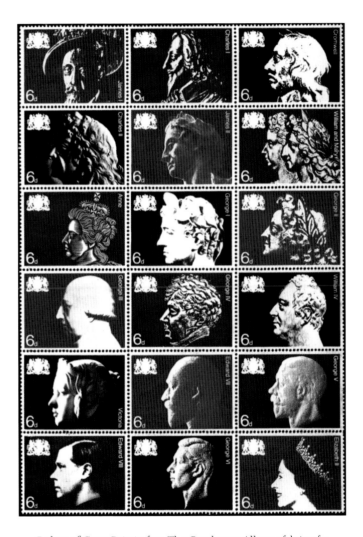

Rulers of Great Britain from The Gentleman Album of *designs for 100 experimental stamps, 1966. This set was essayed, despite its omission of the Queen's head, but not issued.*

century, and G.W. de Saulles' *Britannia* from the 1902 florin. His intertwining of these national figurative symbols in the manner of the double-ended court cards in a pack of playing cards, was so successful that it was used on both sides of the Channel.

The posters he has designed for the National Trust and British Steel, as well as the graphics produced over the last twenty years in aid of campaigns such as the National Trust's protest over the proposed bypass through Petworth Park and his own opposition to the Iraq War, also reflect this suppression of superfluous detail. In one design for the Petworth campaign he managed to eliminate the requirement for any verbal message by the creation of a repeating path of tyre tracks mindlessly bisecting the park, despoiling its tranquility. The image said it all. To achieve this he used a combination of tachism and photography, superimposing a sequence of rubbings from a car tyre onto a photograph of Petworth. Jobs like this taught him to use the camera for specific purposes, but made him aware that though a photograph can be as persuasive as a drawing, it can never have the same individuality.

To the viewer, the shocking image of tyre tracks churning up the beauty of Petworth implied the presence of a totalitarian state riding roughshod over local opinion. For some of his other campaigns Gentleman has used similar shock tactics, combining them with visual humour in order to ram home his message. He has never been afraid to give full rein to his imagination, playing with shapes, images, typography, and the creation of surreal juxtapositions. Witty as these images often are, there is no gainsaying the anger that has driven him to create them: this comes through particularly strongly in *A Special Relationship*, a book charting Anglo-American relations from 1607 to Greenham Common. Here the vandalism implicit in defacing a Bewick engraving, the transformation of Britain and Ireland into a chessboard with missiles substituting for pawns, a Trojan horse defecating nuclear weapons, and the typographic configuration of the letters 'U S' to create the outline of a bare bottom, are all disconcerting. Printed starkly in red and black, they make a powerful political statement. Whatever semantic definitions Gentleman may have made in the past to describe the twin poles of Art and Industry, it is clear from looking at his work as a whole – whether as a book illustrator, muralist, stamp designer, poster artist, political activist or watercolourist – that there are basically no divisions for him, each activity feeds off, and is enriched, by the others. A viewpoint acknowledged in his conclusion to a paper he read recently to the Double Crown Club, when he stated: 'My work has taught me that if any boundaries between art and design indeed exist, they are porous – one can seep through them in either direction, almost without noticing.'

Early in life he made three decisions: he wanted always to work for himself, never to teach and never to commute. Apart from his two years as a junior tutor at the Royal College of Art, he has achieved these objectives and in the process knitted together an apparently seamless life, travelling to remarkable places in order to paint and write about them; designing stamps and symbols, prints and protest placards. Art and design, he says, are part of a spectrum: 'The balance between them may vary, but they are inseparable.'

1. *Artwork*, p.14.
2. Richard Guyatt, ed. *Births, Marriages and Deaths*, London, Lion and Unicorn Press, 1954.
3. Limited Editions Club *Newsletter*, April 1968.
4. David Gentleman, *Design in Miniature*, London, Studio Vista, 1972, p. 7.
5. Introduction to *A Timeless Classic: The Evolution of Machin's Icon*, by Douglas N. Muir, British Postal Museum & Archive, 2007.

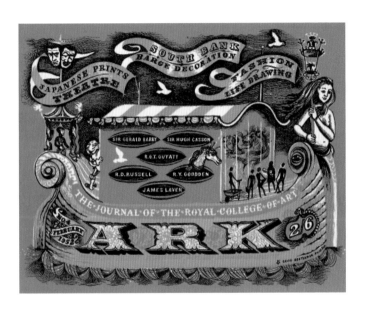

Cover of the fourth issue of Ark, the RCA's unofficial journal, 1952, showing an Ark whose superstructure was the Lion and Unicorn Pavilion at the Festival of Britain, celebrating British idiosyncrasy. It was jointly designed by two RCA professors, Robert Goodden and Richard Guyatt, who hold their plans on deck, right. Ark had been started a year earlier by Jack Stafford. Geoffrey Ireland had drawn earlier covers and John Minton had written a funny and perceptive article warning students of the perils of too-early success.

Cornish Fishing Boat, 1954, one of the third series of lithographs
published by J Lyons and Co, to decorate their chain of teashops. It was
drawn 'to plate' in ten workings and printed at Chromoworks in Willesden.

*Title page from* What About Wine? *by André Simon, Newman Neame, 1954.*

*Wood engravings for Wine List No.1 by Harveys of Bristol, 1961.*

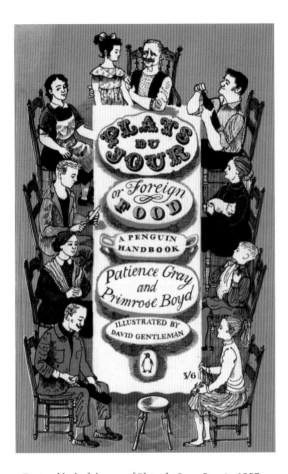

Front and back of the cover of Plats du Jour, Penguin, 1957.
On the front a meal is about to begin; the back shows the table
afterwards. Gentleman drew the people from his own sketches, the
faces from Paris Match photographs; the chairs while staying
in a house in Ramatuelle in the hills above St Tropez. The cover
was drawn as separations and printed in black, pink and grey.

Three Christmas cards for Michael and Felicity Behrens, c1956-8, showing their early Victorian house by the Thames, near Henley. *Above: pen and wash drawing; below: brush-drawn colour separations; above right: wood engraving with two separations.*

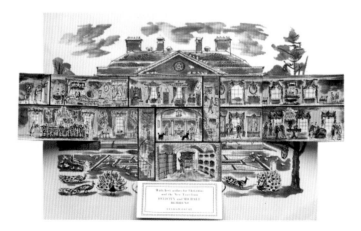

Below: a much later card Gentleman engraved for his own use, c1975.
It shows Smith's Wharf, a long-vanished warehouse on the Thames near
Cannon Street. Only two bays of the building were engraved; proofs were
then pasted up to make the complete building.

*Above*: Covent Garden mug for David Mellor Ltd, 1983. *Pen drawing of the recently renovated Dedicated Market. Photolitho transfer with overlaid colour separations in grey, yellow and brown. Opposite: Glazed chintz furnishing fabric* Essex Coast *commissioned by Alastair Morton for Edinburgh Weavers, c1967. Fountain pen drawings of the waterfront at Manningtree, Essex.*

*Above*: Ashdown House, *one of a set of watercolours of castles and great houses commissioned as dinner plates by Wedgwood in the early seventies.*

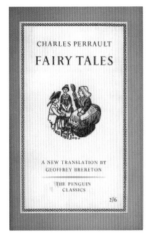

*Wood engravings for Penguin Classics and Pelican, c1954-6.*

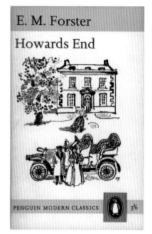

Drawings for Penguin Modern Classics, c1956-8.

Visitors' London, *posters for London Transport, 1957.*

### WESTMINSTER ABBEY

Beneath this lattern of England's honour he her most famous dead. Near, hanging in Henry VII's Chapel, beneath a soaring roof of unsurpassed magnificence, the banners of the Order of the Bath. Henry himself lies here with his queen, and in the east end stands the Battle of Britain memorial window. In every corner of the Abbey lies history to come.

### THE TOWER OF LONDON

Ask a Yeoman Warder in his gay Tudor scarlet anything you like about its long grim history. Dimly, your eyes with the Green Jewels; stroll on Tower Green, unheeded by the famous ravens strutting fatly black upon the lawn, or walk beside the river and how is lapping darkly past Traitor's Gate.

### LONDON RIVER

Stand on Tower Bridge and see the finest of ports in the Pool of London. Wander east on the north bank through the seafaring borough of Wapping. From these reaches Elizabethan ships sail for the Northern Seas. From here the great merchant companies established their rich trade with India and the East. Here the very cradle of Britain's commercial empire.

### THE GUARDS

An essential ingredient in London's pageantry. The Guardsman, seemingly erect before the gates of Buckingham Palace and St. James's. The Household Cavalry, facing unperturbed the roar of Whitehall's traffic and the admiring audience at the horse's feet. The Changing of the Guard remains unchallenged as London's finest free show, with all the usual splendour of time-honoured ceremonial.

FREE LEAFLETS are published by London Transport. In one you will find full details about the Changing of the Guard and when and where best to see it. Others list museums, art galleries and historic houses open to the public. And there are maps of bus and Underground services to help you find your way. All can be had free from the Public Relations Officer, 55 Broadway, Westminster, S.W.1.

Illustrations for The Swiss Family Robinson, Limited Editions
Club of New York, 1963. Wood engravings with brush-drawn colour.

The Swiss Family Robinson's well-appointed tree house, which used up some of
the debris from the shipwreck, was inspired by memories of rickety tree shacks in the
Gentleman garden, built by a wartime evacuee in a small sycamore tree poised over
the river Beane.

Spreads and illustrations for The Jungle Book, Limited Editions Club of New York, 1968. Pen drawings with colour, lithographed on grained film.

*Covers for* The New Penguin Shakespeare *series, 1968-75. Wood engravings, some enlarged, with two- or three-colour overlays cut from plastic film.*

New Penguin Shakespeare

# Macbeth

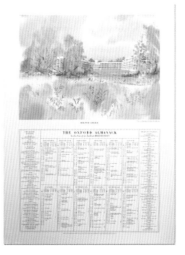

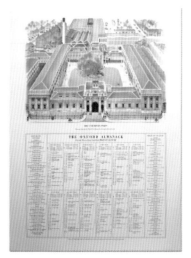

Four University Almanacs for the Oxford University Press, 1966-9.
Pen and watercolour

Covers and spreads from Fenella in Ireland, Cape, 1968, watercolour. One of four
children's books about holidays – others were set in Greece, Spain and the South of France.

Corporate identity for the British Steel Corporation, 1970.
The two elements of the symbol represent steel samples bent
to demonstrate their flexibility under stress.

Symbols for two publishers, The Bodley Head, 1970 and Duckworth, c1970;
for the Bodleian Library, Oxford, 1992 and 2002; for a Duckworth classical
series, showing Penelope at her loom, after Holbein, c1972; for the finance
house Compagnie Financiere et du Credit SA of Lausanne; and for a series of
science books published by Cambridge University Press, c1974.

Spread from 'The inspired plagiarism of Stanford White' a feature for New York
Magazine on the Manhattan buildings of the versatile American architect Stanford
White of the firm McKim, Mead and White.

White's best known buildings included The Washington Square Arch, opposite,
The Racquet and Tennis Club, above, The Harvard Club and The Villard Building,
below. These drawings were made during a visit to New York in 1972.

Booklet cover and poster Victorian London for
London Transport, c 1973. For this respectful act of
homage to Victorian architecture, Gentleman drew
the buildings mechanically with a Rotring pen and
then uncharacteristically tinted them in decorative
rather then realistic colours. The blue and green
facades at either side were drawn in plain elevation
and then photographed in perspective.

Illustrations for the traditional Christmas mummers' play St George and the Dragon, *Atheneum*, New York 1973, wood engravings with overlays in two colours. The costumes were based on drawings of mummers in the English Folk Dance and Song Society archive.

Covers for company annual reports and accounts for Harveys of Bristol Ltd, 1963,
Prudential Assurance, 1982 and 1983, and Credit Mutuel, Paris, 1997.

*Covers for* Esso Magazine, 1961, ICI Magazine, 1975, British Medical
Journal, 1982, *and* London Review of Books, c1979.

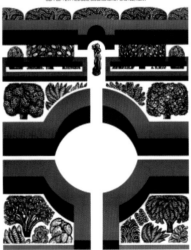

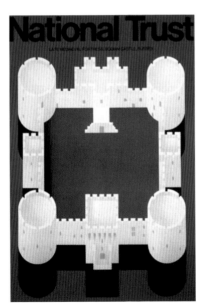

Opposite: Posters; Ickworth Volute, Cornish Beam Engine, Sissinghurst Castle, Bodiam Castle for the National Trust, 1972. Above: Gentleman took the photographs for many National Trust posters, including the two above for tree appeals — one dramatic, the other calm — 1975 and 1987. The wood engraved symbol below is a botanically more accurate redesign of an already familiar device.

Two campaigning National Trust posters, Petworth Tyretracks and Petworth Say No!, 1976. Photomontages of Petworth House and Park.

The posters were designed to arouse public opposition to a proposed bypass through
Petworth Park, made famous by Turner's paintings. The scheme was abandoned.

*Wood engravings for press advertisments for the DuPont pesticide Benlate, early 1970s. This pesticide was later*

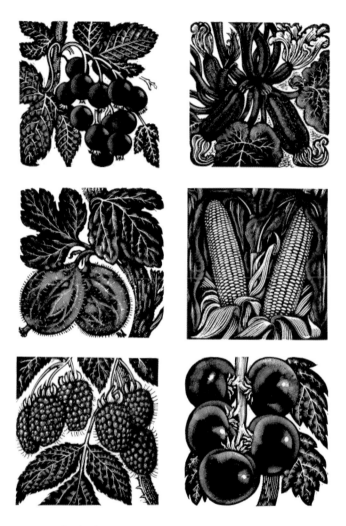

found to have caused blindness in its users; Gentleman did
no more work for DuPont, and no more engraved adverts.

Everyday Architecture in Towns, 1976 one of a series of four RIBA wallcharts,

*published to mark European Architectural Heritage Year. Watercolour drawings.*

Jackets using wood engravings or typography for Duckworth, publishers of mainly academic books. Its energetic and scholarly chairman, Colin Haycraft, was Gentleman's neighbour and lived three doors down to Gentleman's left; his office was further up the street to the right, he commissioned these jackets on his way to work, c1970.

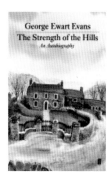  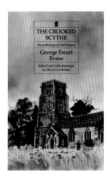

*Jackets for Faber books, 1975-1990s, watercolour drawings. They included Durrell's Alexandria quartet and Avignon quintet, Sassoon's autobiographical novels about the 1914-18 war, and George Ewart Evans' books combining sociology with oral history. In 1968 Gentleman marrried Evans' daughter, Sue.*

Social Reformers postage stamps for Royal Mail, commemorating the pioneering work of the factory owner Robert Owen, the philanthropist Lord Shaftesbury, the prison reformer Elizabeth Fry and the miners' trade union leader Thomas Hepburn, 1976.

Gentleman's first stamp, for National Productivity Year, 1962, had to include the central arrow device, so he adapted it as the main motif. For the more minimal Concorde, 1969, he again overprinted two colours to make a third.

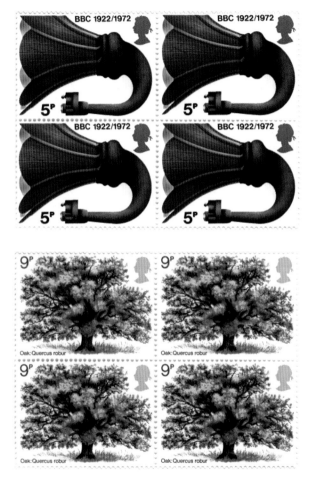

The designs for the BBC, 1972 and the Oak Tree, 1973, each a single image, one as a symbol, the other as a picture. The oak tree's five printings were drawn as individual separations, as if making a colour lithograph.

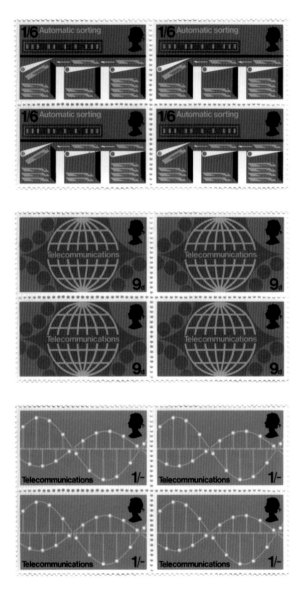

*Repeat pattern stamps symbolising technological advances in post and telecoms, 1969. These, with the National Giro, all then still formed part of the Post Office.*

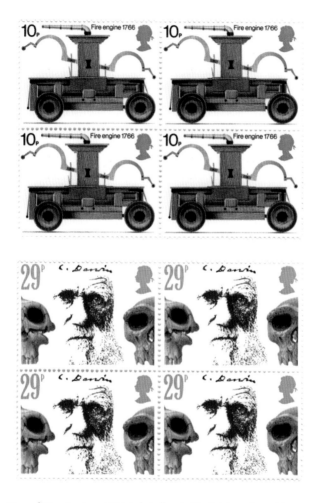

Manual Fire Engine, 1974, *technically primitive but drawn here with mechanical precision. Above,* Charles Darwin, 1982, *flanked by the skulls of two individuals he acknowledged as his prehistoric ancestors. The photograph of Darwin is untouched but is bleached out to leave a clear background for the skulls.*

The Charing Cross mural had to incorporate such items as the station's name, the London Transport logo, telephones and receptacles for staff letters, benches for seating, and entrances, exits, and passages through to the adjoining platform. Rather than allowing them to become nuisances, the design was built around these features: the benches for example were used not only by the travelling public but also by the figures in the mural. Fearing possible graffiti, Gentleman was reassured by Sid Hardy, London Transport's Chief Architect, that if the public were treated with respect, it would respond in kind. To be on the safe side, however, Hardy also ordered ample supplies of

solvent, and any graffiti have been quickly cleaned off. In any case, they had always looked pretty puny against the heavy black lines of the engravings.

Previous page: Charing Cross underground station, 1979: original design showing how the original cross was built, from quarrying the stone to positioning the final pinnacle. David Gentleman's wood engravings were photographed, enlarged twenty times and screen-printed onto impregnated paper which was then laminated and fixed to a curved former.

Illustrations for The Dancing Tigers by Russell Hoban, Cape, 1979.
Watercolour and crayon. While in India a decade earlier, Gentleman had stayed
in a disused hunting lodge in The Jungle Book's Seoni hills and had walked

through a few miles of dry jungle, but had come across no tigers. He drew the
ones above after repeated visits to London Zoo, which in the seventies still had
a good stock of them and was only ten minutes' walk from his studio.

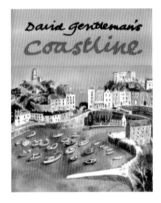

*Jackets and spreads from Gentleman's books on* Britain, 1982, London, 1985, *the* British Coastline, 1988 (*Weidenfeld*), Paris, 1991, India, 1994 *and* Italy, 1997, (*John Curtis/Hodder Headline*).

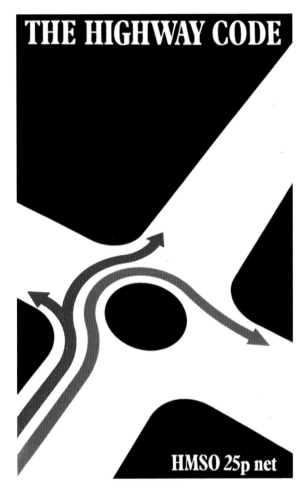

Cover of The Highway Code, 1978. The artwork was prepared using Letrafilm, an adhesive coloured plastic film, stuck lightly down and cut with a scalpel taped to a pair of compasses. The unwanted areas peeled off. The finished image was then photographed from an angle to suggest an aerial perspective.

Bodleian Library symbol, 1992, refined and adapted for its quatercentenary in 2002. Below: Corporate Seal of the House of Lords, 1992.

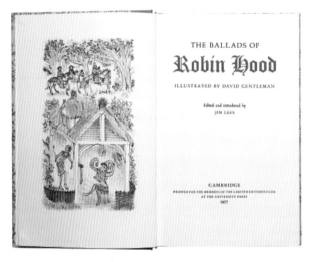

*Illustrations for* The Ballads of Robin Hood, *Limited Editions Club,1977.*
*Black pen drawings with six-colour lithography drawn on zinc plates.*

*Poster for an exhibition of lithographs of Covent Garden, published by Christina Smith's Seven Dials Press in 1980. Lithograph, quickly drawn on a zinc plate balanced on a car roof in Langley Street, Covent Garden.*

**A SPECIAL RELATIONSHIP**
DAVID GENTLEMAN

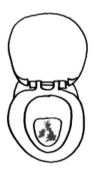

A Special Relationship, *Faber, 1987.* This 64-page commentary on the
*Anglo-American alliance includes drawings, designs, old engravings, photomontages
and a few dates, but no words. Gentleman's photograph (below, with additions) had
originally been used as a seat-back panel on the Bakerloo* Line platforms in
*Charing Cross underground station.*

# Bliar

Stop the War Coalition www.stopwar.org.uk 020 7053 2153/4/5/6

# n more lies

Stop the War Coalition www.stopwar.org.uk 020 7053 2153/4/5/6 Designed by David Gentleman Printed by East End Offset Ltd (TU) London E3 ☎ 020 7538 2521

Two march placards for the Stop the War Coalition, 2003-8, protesting against the invasion of Iraq. Opposite: 100,000 drops of blood, an installation in Parliament Square in February 2006, three years after the war began. Each drop represented someone – Iraqi, American or British – who had died in Iraq because of the invasion.

When early in 2003 the invasion of Iraq seemed imminent, Gentleman offered the Stop the War Coalition the design for a blood-spattered march placard saying 'No'. 5,000 of them were carried on 15 February by marchers on the biggest demonstration in British political history. He went on to design many others in similar vein throughout the war, all incorporating in various ways the blood-stain motif as part of the typography.

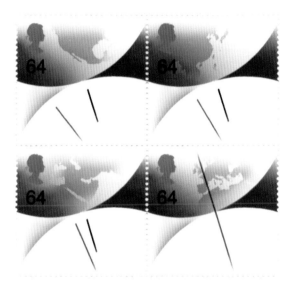

A set of four se-tenant stamps issued to mark the instant at which the twentieth century became the twenty-first. Their theme is the passage of time, symbolised by the cusp between two arcs. The horizontal wave passing across from stamp to stamp represents time's continuity; the earth's rotation is the way we measure it, whether in days, years or millennia; a moving hand on a clockface makes its passing visible.

Six low-value coin designs for Royal Mint, 2007, featuring the oak tree as a time-honoured national icon. Its growth from acorn to mature tree, reflected in the increasing denominations, also suggests change and a developing nation with a growing concern for the environment. These coins were not issued.

Five pound coin for the Royal Mint, 2002, commemorating the
Entente Cordiale. The coin, giving equal prominence to Britannia
and her French counterpart Marianne, was simultaneously issued
by the French Monnaie. Below: Two pound coin for the Royal Mint,
2007, commemorating the bicentenary of the 1807 Act for the
Abolition of the Slave Trade within the British Empire.

# Chronology

| | | |
|---|---|---|
| 1930 | Born London; parents move to Hertford. | |
| 1939 | Hertford Grammar School. | |
| 1947-8 | St Albans School of Art. | |
| 1948-50 | National Service: Salisbury Plain, Cornwall. | |
| 1950 | Mural *Barnet Fair* in new Hertfordshire school. | |
| 1950-3 | Royal College of Art (School of Graphic Design). | |
| 1951 | Changes from Graphic Design to Illustration course; taught by Edward Bawden and John Nash. | |
| 1952 | Ceramic plates *Hampton Court*. | |
| 1953 | Marries Rosalind Dease. | |
| 1952-3 | Posters for 1953 *Orphée*, RCA Diploma Exhibition. | |
| 1953-5 | Junior tutor at RCA; starts freelancing. | |
| 1955-9 | Early Penguin covers: *Mountain Inn*, *Passage to India*, *Howards End*. | |
| 1957 | *Visitors' London* poster for London Transport. | |
| 1956-7 | Fabrics for Edinburgh Weavers: *Essex*, *Stradetta*, *Provencal*. | |
| 1957 | Illustrations for *Plats du Jour*, Penguin. | |
| 1957-60s | Drawings for *House & Garden*. | |
| 1958 | Wallpaper designs for Wallpaper Manufacturers Ltd. | |
| 1957-9 | Counties watercolours for Shell press advertisements. | |
| 1960-1 | Drawings of *Changing London* | |

(with Robert Harling) for the *Sunday Times*.

| | |
|---|---|
| 1961 | Engraved press advertisements for launch of the *Sunday Telegraph* |
| 1961 | Illustrations with overlays for *Bridges on the Backs*, Cambridge University Press. |
| 1961 | Engraving for Harveys of Bristol company report. |
| 1962 | First stamp, *National Productivity Year*. |
| 1963 | Engraved illustrations for *The Swiss Family Robinson*. |
| 1964 | Engravings for *The Shepherd's Calendar*, Oxford University Press. |
| 1964 | *Shakespeare Festival* stamps. |
| 1965 | *Churchill* stamps. |
| 1965 | *Battle of Britain* stamps. |
| 1966 | *Battle of Hastings* stamps. |
| 1966 | Stamps and design proposals for *The Gentleman Album*. |
| 1966-90s | Illustrations for George Ewart Evans's oral history books. |
| 1966 | Four children's books, starting with *Fenella in Ireland*. |
| 1966-70s | Four *Oxford Almanacs* for Oxford University Press. |
| 1967 | Goes to India as government guest to research *The Jungle Books*. |
| 1968 | Illustrations for *The Jungle Books*. |
| 1968 | Marries Susan Evans. |
| 1969 | *Prince of Wales Investiture* stamps. |

| | | | |
|---|---|---|---|
| 1969 | British Ships stamps. | 1983 | Earthenware mug Covent Garden for David Mellor. |
| 1969 | First Suite of lithographs. | | |
| 1969 | Concorde stamps. | 1985 | David Gentleman's London published by Weidenfeld. |
| 1969 | Post Office Technology stamps. | | |
| 1969 | Philympia stamps. | 1987 | A Special Relationship published by Faber. |
| 1970s | First wood engraving covers for New Penguin Shakespeare. | 1988 | David Gentleman's Coastline published by Weidenfeld. |
| 1970-2007 | Exhibitions of watercolours at Mercury Gallery and Fine Art Society. | c.1988 | 250,000 trees lost poster for National Trust. |
| 1972 | Design in Miniature published by Studio Vista. | 1989 | Ely Cathedral stamps. |
| | | 1991 | David Gentleman's Paris published by Hodder Headline. |
| 1972 | Fortifications screenprints. | | |
| 1972 | BBC 1922-72 postage stamps. | 1993 | Abbotsbury Swans stamps. |
| 1972 | Drawings of Stanford White's buildings for New York Magazine. | 1994 | David Gentleman's India published by Hodder Headline. |
| 1973 | Oak Tree stamp. | 1997 | David Gentleman's Italy published by Hodder Headline. |
| 1974 | Fire Engines stamps. | | |
| 1975 | Everyday Architecture wallcharts for RIBA. | c1998 | Posters for Greenpeace. |
| | | 1999 | Millennium Timekeeper stamps. |
| 1976 | Social Reformers stamps. | 2000 | Wood Engravings of David Gentleman published by David Esslemont. |
| 1977 | Twelve Days of Christmas stamps. | | |
| 1977 | Illustrations for Robin Hood. | 2002 | Artwork published by Ebury Press. |
| 1978 | Stamps for the Republic of Nauru. | | |
| | | 2002 | Entente Cordiale coin for Royal Mint. |
| 1978 | Cover for Highway Code. | | |
| 1980 | Completion of New Penguin Shakespeare covers. | 2003-8 | March placards for Stop the War. |
| | | 2005 | Installation 100,000 drops of blood in Parliament Square, London. |
| 1979 | Eleanor Cross Mural, Charing Cross underground station. | | |
| | | 2005 | Abolition of Slavery coin for Royal Mint. |
| 1982 | Charles Darwin stamps. | | |
| 1982 | David Gentleman's Britain published by Weidenfeld. | Page 96 | Camden Town Youth, 2008 |